Beginning Fun With Crayons

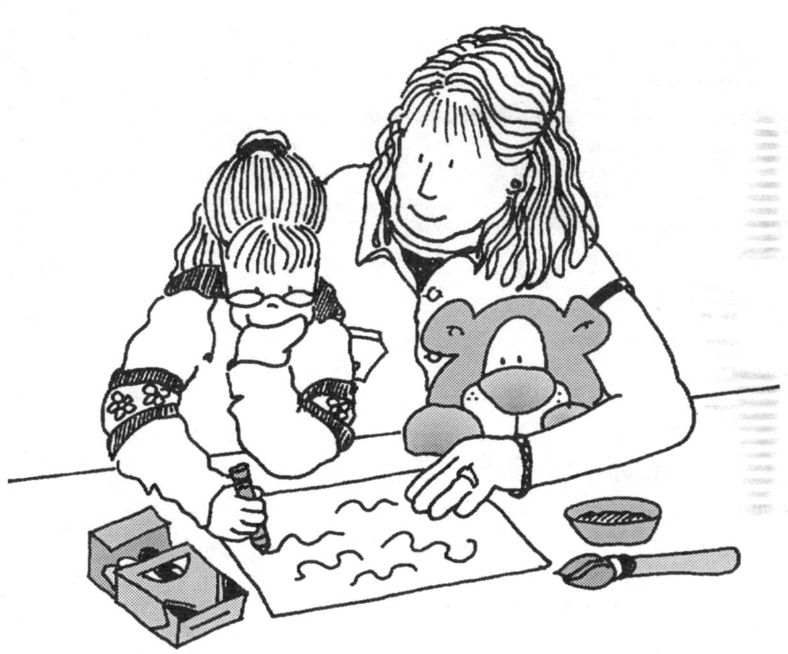

Written and Compiled by Elizabeth McKinnon
Illustrated by Marion Hopping Ekberg

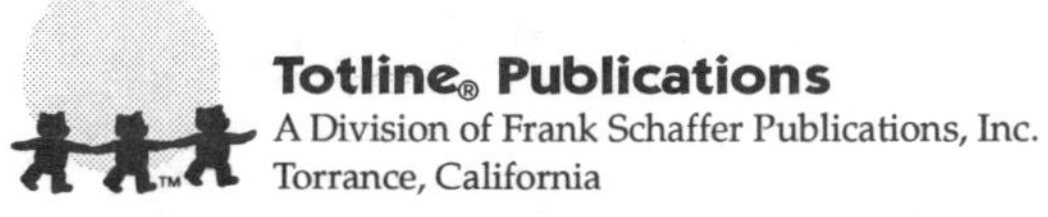

Totline® Publications
A Division of Frank Schaffer Publications, Inc.
Torrance, California

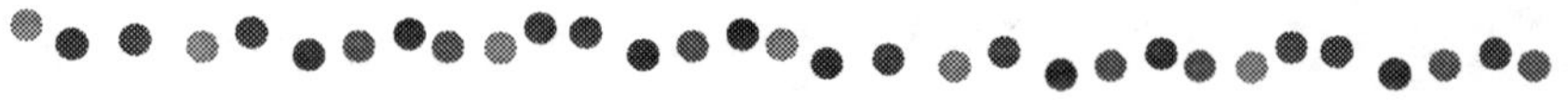

Totline® Publications would like to acknowledge the following childcare professionals for contributing some of the activities in this book: Sr. Mary Bezold, Corbin, KY; Carole Hardy, Pittsburgh, PA; Cathy Herring, Cincinnati, OH; Colraine Pettipaw Hunley, Doylestown, PA; Kathy Monahan, Coon Rapids, MN; Beverly Qualheim, Manitowoc, WI; Betty Silkunas, Lansdale, PA; Jane M. Spannbauer, So. St. Paul, MN; Betty Loew White, South Beechwold, OH; JoAnn Wilson, Boise, ID.

Managing Editor: Kathleen Cubley
Editors: Gayle Bittinger, Carol Gnojewski, Susan Hodges, Jean Warren
Copyeditor: Kris Fulsaas
Proofreader: Miriam Bulmer
Editorial Assistant: Durby Peterson
Graphic Designer (cover): Brenda Mann Harrison
Graphic Designer: Sarah Ness
Production Assistant: Melody Olney

ISBN 1-57029-134-9

Printed in the United States of America
Published by Totline® Publications
Editorial Office: P.O. Box 2250
Everett, WA 98203
Business Office: 23740 Hawthorne Blvd.
Torrance, CA 90505

20 19 18 17 16 15 14 13 12 11 10 9 8 7 6 5 4 3 2

Art plays an important part in developing your child's readiness to learn. Your role is to provide art opportunities, along with materials you probably already have on hand.

Whenever your child wants to draw a picture, chances are the first materials you offer are crayons and paper. Crayons are inexpensive, easy to find, and very satisfying to use.

Beginning Fun With Crayons opens with some crayon tips and a list of different papers and other materials that your child can use to color on. It goes on to provide suggestions for helping your child try such projects as crayon rubbings, crayon resist pictures, and crayon melts. The book concludes with ideas for using crayons to make simple toys and seasonal art that your child is sure to enjoy.

Start the fun now by setting out crayons and paper. Then open to one of the activities on the following pages, and let the art adventures begin.

Happy coloring!

A Word About Safety: The activities in *Beginning Fun With Crayons* are appropriate for young children between the ages of 2 and 5. However, keep in mind that if a project calls for using small objects, an adult should supervise at all times to make sure that children do not put the objects in their mouth. It is recommended that you use art materials that are specifically labeled as safe for children unless the materials are to be used only by an adult. Also, several of the activities in this book require the use of an electric iron. Remember that close supervision is necessary when any appliance is used near young children.

Crayon Tips

Crayons are sure to be a basic staple whenever you put together art supplies for your young child. Here are some crayon tips that you may find helpful.

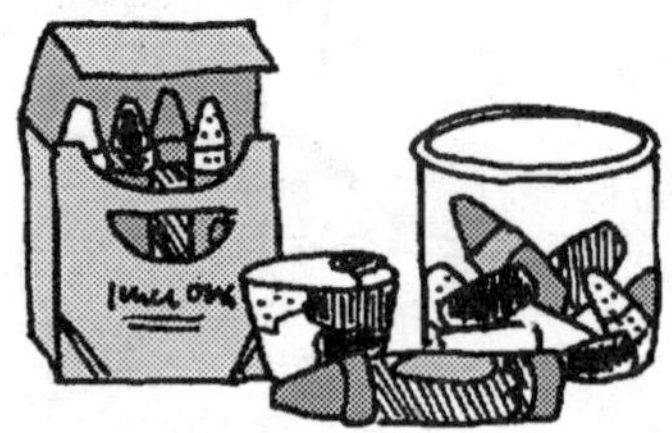

- When shopping for crayons, check variety stores, art and crafts stores, or any place where school supplies are sold. Look for ordinary crayons, jumbo crayons, washable crayons, glitter crayons, scented crayons, and so on.
- Provide toddlers with jumbo crayons for drawing and coloring. They are easier for little fingers to control.
- To help keep new crayons from breaking, wrap them with masking tape. Peel off the tape layers as the crayons wear down.
- Save old or broken crayon pieces in a special container. Remove the paper wrappers, and the crayons are ready for making rubbings. Or, use the crayon bits for the Giant Crayons activity on page 6.
- Store crayons in empty peanut butter jars. The see-through containers make finding the desired colors easy.
- For a personal crayon holder your child is sure to like, store a selection of colors in a metal bandage box with a lid.
- To extend art time into bath time, look for soap crayons in bath shops. Your child can draw colored designs on the bottom and sides of the tub, and they will wash away in a flash.
- If the worst should happen and your child colors on a wall, try this homemade crayon remover. Make a paste of baking soda and water. Then, using a sponge, gently rub the paste over the crayon marks until they disappear.

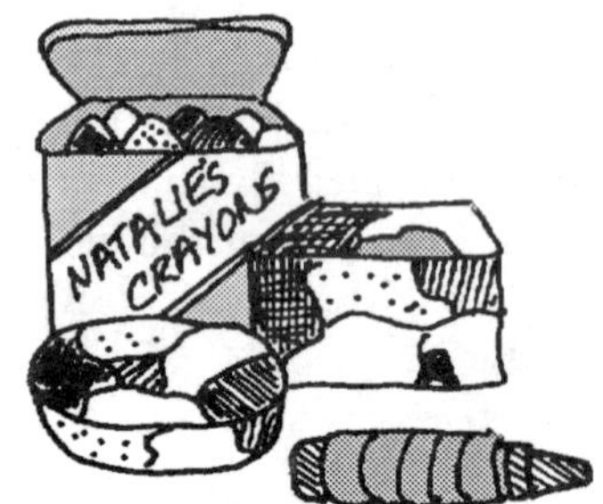

Materials to Color On

For basic coloring, all your child needs is a piece of white paper and crayons. But why not enrich her art experience by providing a variety of materials to color on? Below are some to try.

- old newspapers
- brown grocery bags
- corrugated cardboard
- paper plates
- computer paper
- junk mail
- used gift-wrap
- outdated calendar pages
- heavy-duty paper towels
- cardboard tubes
- sandpaper
- wood scraps
- cardboard egg cartons
- outdated phone book pages
- cardboard boxes
- copy shop throwaways

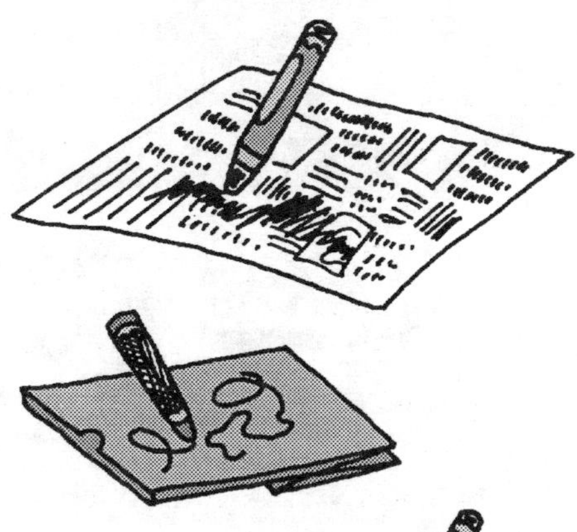

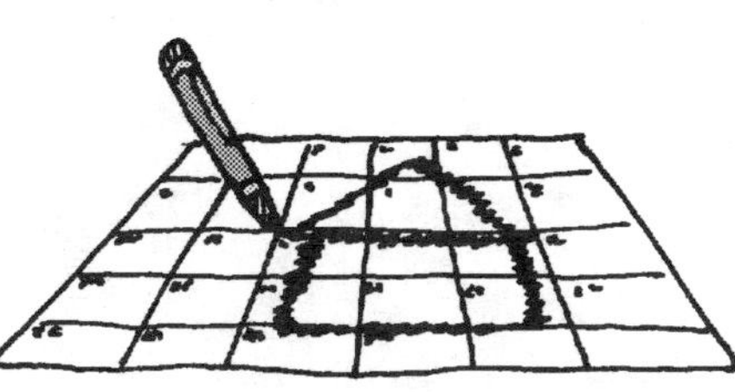

Look around your home for other materials your child can enjoy coloring on.

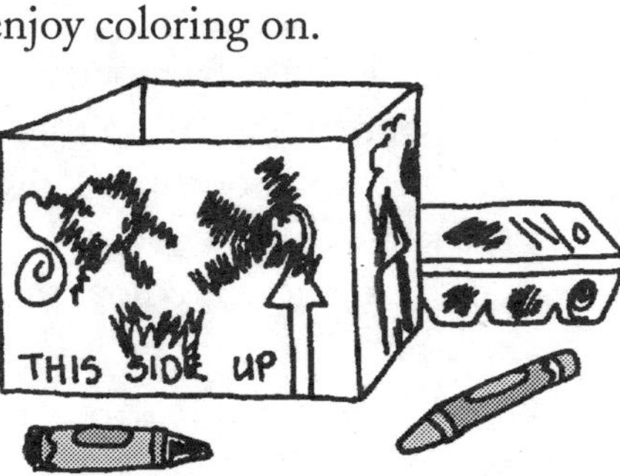

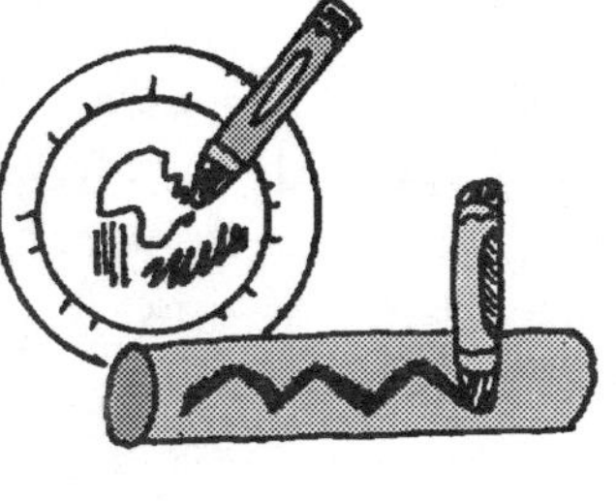

Crayon Combos

Why do ordinary coloring when you can create in new ways? Here are two ideas to try.

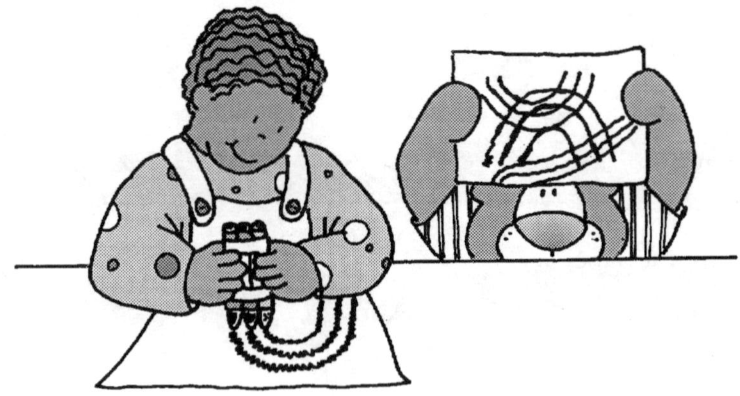

Rainbow Crayons—Find two or more different-colored crayons that are approximately the same length. Line them up with the points all facing in the same direction. Using masking tape, fasten the crayons together in a row. Then show your child how to hold the crayons and draw designs with them on paper. Encourage him to try making rainbow arcs.

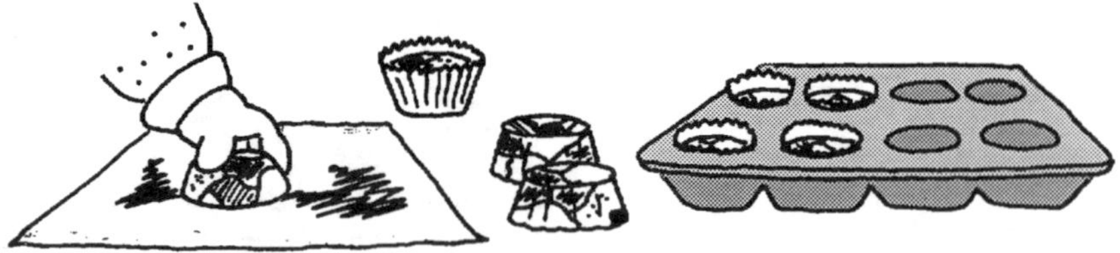

Giant Crayons—Collect old, broken crayons with wrappers removed and sort them by color into separate piles. Chop the crayons into 1/4-inch pieces. Place foil liners in a muffin tin and fill each liner with crayon pieces of the same color. Put the tin in a 250°F oven until the crayon pieces have melted. Allow the crayons to cool and then peel off the foil liners. Give the "giants" to your child to use for coloring projects.

Crayon Rubbings

Half the fun of making rubbings is looking for textured items to use. For starters, choose several different coins and attach them to a tabletop with loops of tape rolled sticky side out. Give your child a piece of lightweight paper such as typing paper or newsprint. Show her how to place the paper on top of the coins and color over them with the side of a peeled crayon to make the raised designs appear. Help her move the paper to a new position and make more rubbings with a different-colored crayon. Then, starting with fresh paper, continue the activity using other objects such as keys, combs, corrugated cardboard, paper clips, rubber bands, or embossed greeting cards.

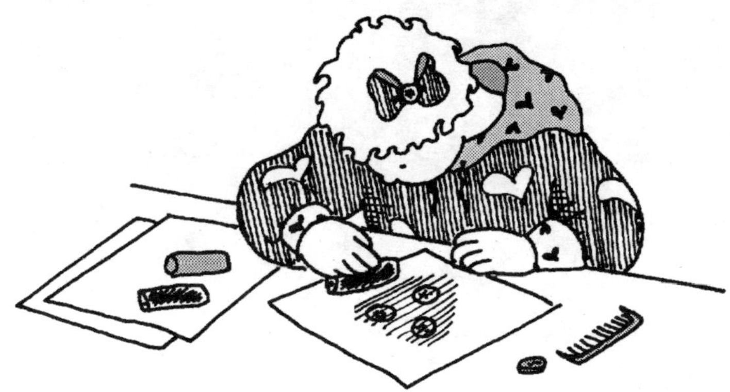

For More Fun

Take crayons and paper outdoors, and encourage your child to search for objects and surfaces that would make interesting rubbings. Some suggestions are leaves, feathers, grass, tree trunks, sidewalks, and metal grates.

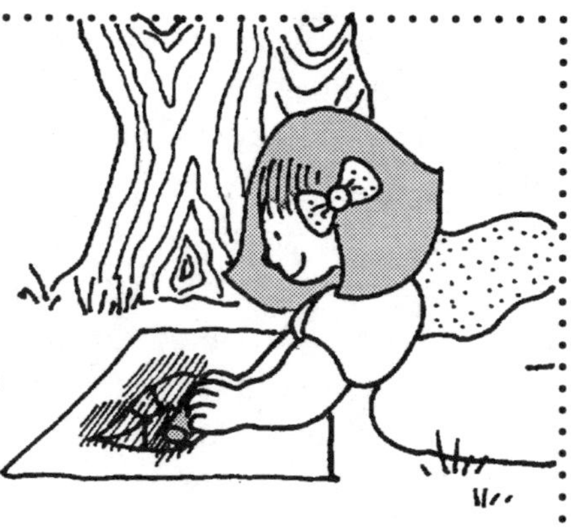

Crayon Stencils

Creating with stencils makes this activity especially fun. Select a cookie cutter or a coloring book picture to use as a pattern. Trace the pattern onto a piece of thin cardboard or an old file folder. Using a craft knife, cut out the shape. (Put aside the shape cutout to use in the For More Fun activity below.) Tape the piece of cardboard over a piece of plain white paper. Then show your child how to use the side of a peeled crayon to shade over the edges of the cut-out shape in the cardboard. When he has finished, help him remove the piece of cardboard to reveal the stenciled picture that he has made.

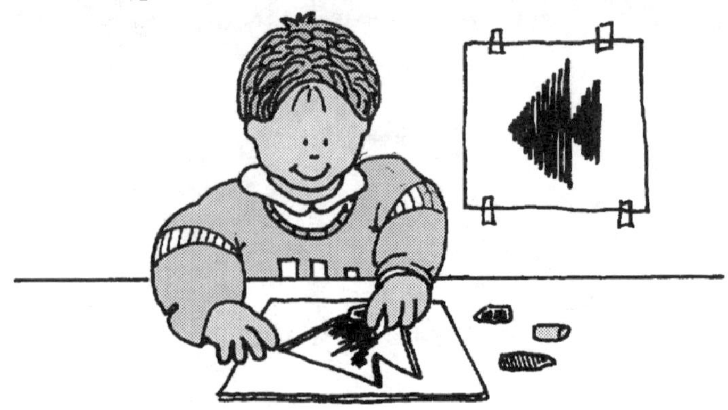

For More Fun

For a different kind of stencil activity, use the shape cutout from the activity above, or cut out a geometric shape, such as a triangle or a square, from thin cardboard. Use pieces of masking tape rolled sticky side out to attach the shape to the center of a large piece of white paper. Let your child color over the edges of the shape, using the side of a peeled crayon. Then show him how to remove the taped-on shape to reveal his stenciled picture.

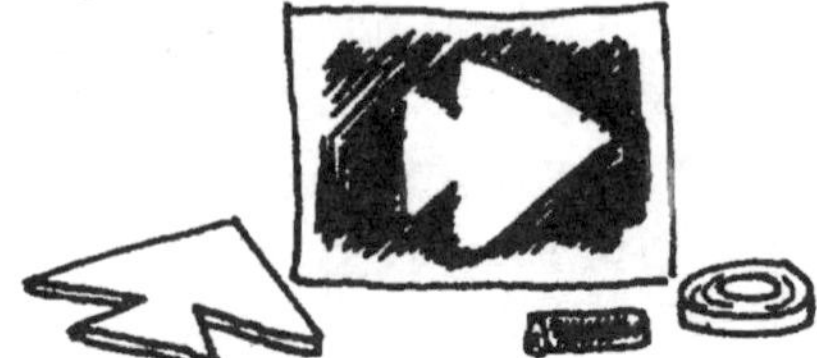

Crayon Prints

Making prints like the ones below can be surprising and magical for your child.

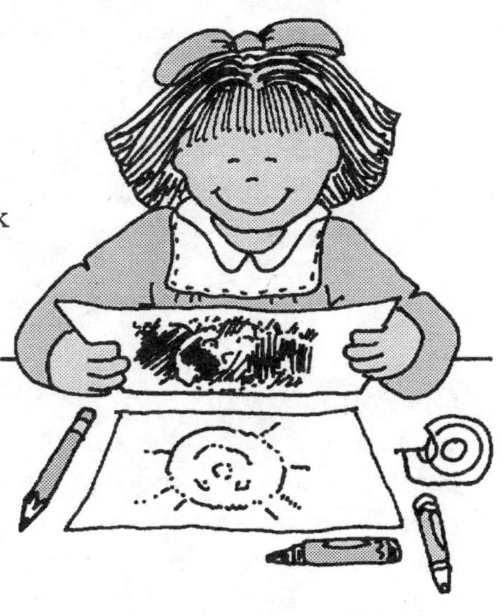

Crayon Transfer Printing—Help your child color all over a piece of white construction paper, pressing down firmly and trying not to leave any blank spaces. When the paper is covered with a thick coating of crayon, turn it over and tape it on top of a piece of plain white paper that you have placed on a table. Then let your child use a pencil or a ballpoint pen to draw designs on the back of the crayon-colored paper. When she has finished, help her remove the taped-on paper to reveal the colored prints of her designs that have been transferred to the paper underneath.

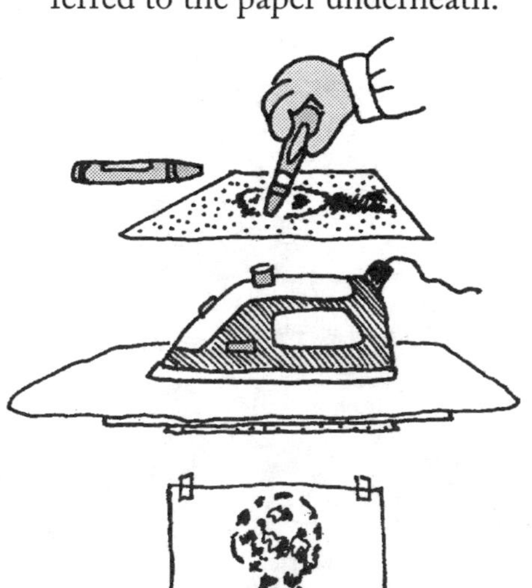

Sandpaper Printing—Invite your child to use bright colors of crayons to draw a picture on a piece of fine or medium grain sandpaper. Place the sandpaper on a flat surface, with the drawing side up, and cover it with a piece of white paper. Put a dishcloth on top of both papers and have your child observe as you press over them with a warm iron. When the cloth has cooled, help your child remove it to discover the dotted crayon print of her sandpaper picture on the piece of white paper.

Crayon Resist

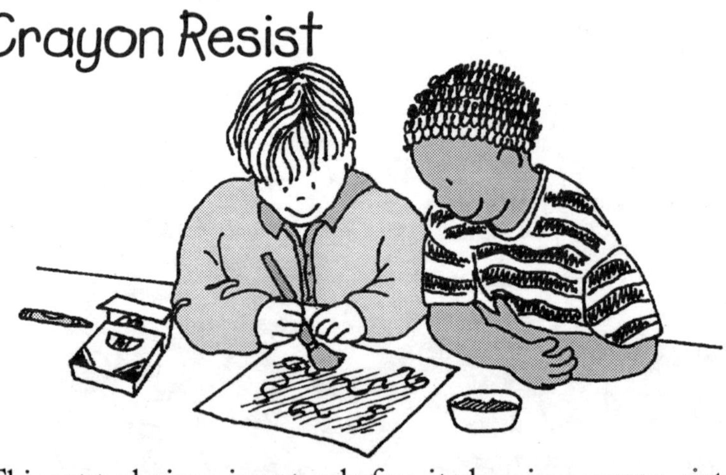

This art technique is not only fun, it also gives crayon pictures a more finished look. Provide your child with a piece of white construction paper and some crayons. Invite him to fill the paper with crayon squiggles to represent fish. (Encourage him to press down firmly while he is coloring.) Meanwhile, make a blue wash by thinning blue tempera paint with water. When your child has finished coloring, show him how to use a paintbrush to cover his paper with the wash. As he does so, the "fish" will appear to be swimming in a big, blue ocean. Another idea to try is "birds" or "butterflies" flying in a blue sky.

For More Fun

Secretly use a white crayon to draw stars and a moon on a piece of white construction paper. (Be sure to press down firmly while coloring.) Make a blue or black wash with tempera paint and water. Then let your child paint the wash over the paper to reveal your "mystery picture."

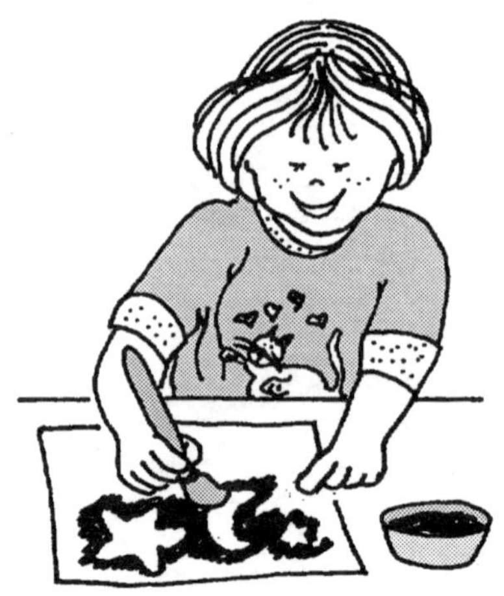

Crayon Melts

You can use this activity idea to make unusual sun catchers for window decorations. Tear off two pieces of waxed paper. Help your child use a kitchen grater to grate crayon shavings onto one of the waxed paper pieces. Let her place tiny pieces of torn colored paper and aluminum foil on top of the shavings. Place the second piece of waxed paper over the first piece and cover both papers with a dishtowel. Then let your child observe as you press a warm iron over the towel to make the waxed paper pieces and the crayon shavings melt together. Help your child cut her transparent creation into an interesting shape such as a heart or a flower. Then display the shape in a sunny window.

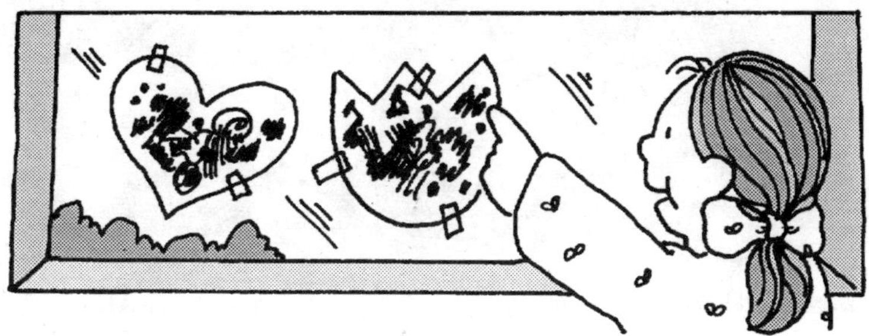

For More Fun

Instead of cutting the fused papers into a special shape, make a frame for the papers by cutting a large shape, such as a heart or a flower, out of the center of a bright color of construction paper. Then help your child tape or staple the fused pieces of waxed paper to the back of the frame to make a see-through picture.

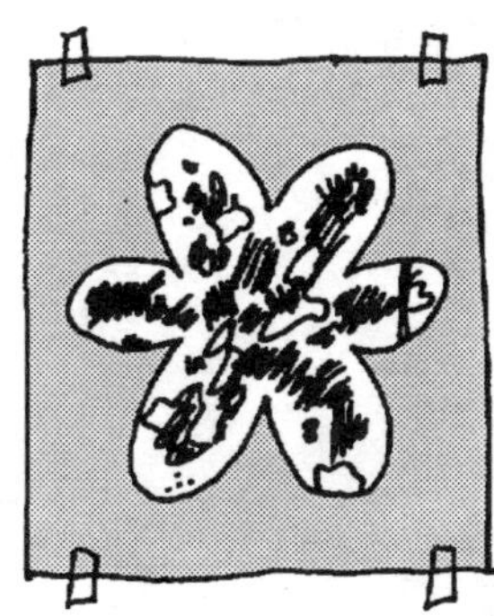

Crayon Toys

You and your child will find that these toys are easy to make and fun to play with.

Colorful Water Bottle—Find a clear-plastic soft-drink bottle with a screw-on cap. Fill the bottle about halfway with water. Help your child use a kitchen grater to grate different-colored crayon shavings onto a piece of paper. Together, drop the shavings into the bottle. Screw on the bottle cap and secure it with strong glue or tape. Then invite your child to shake the bottle and watch the crayon shavings create designs as they float to the top of the water.

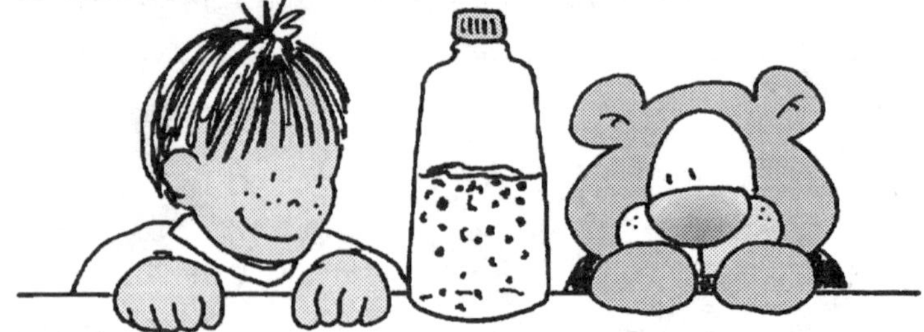

Erasable Coloring Slate—Cover a piece of white cardboard with clear self-stick paper to make an erasable slate. Give the slate to your child and encourage her to color on it with crayons. When it's time to erase the designs, give your child a dry cloth or paper towel to rub over the crayon marks. Her slate will then be ready to use again.

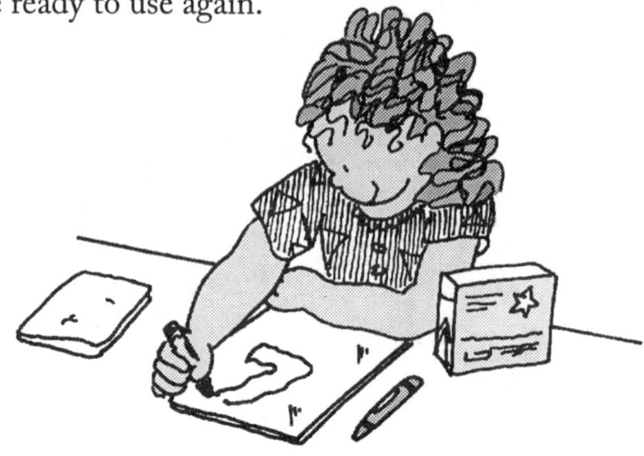

Valentine Hearts—Cut two identical heart shapes out of white construction paper. Help your child use a kitchen grater to grate red crayon shavings onto one of the hearts. Place the second heart on top of the first one and cover both hearts with a dishtowel. Press a warm iron over the towel to melt the crayon shavings. Then show your child how to peel the hearts apart to reveal the crayon designs on both papers.

Easter Basket—Cut a simple basket shape out of bright-colored construction paper. Cut egg shapes out of white paper. Encourage your child to decorate the eggs with crayon designs. When he has finished, help him glue the eggs onto the basket shape.

Summer Snake Mobile—Let your child use crayons to color designs on both sides of a thin paper plate. Help her cut the plate around and around in a spiral so that when you are finished, it resembles a snake. Encourage your child to draw on an eye. Then attach a piece of string to the snake's head for hanging the mobile.